A New True Book

NUMBERS

By Philip Carona

This "true book" was prepared
under the direction of
Illa Podendorf,
formerly with the Laboratory School,
University of Chicago

CHILDRENS PRESS, CHICAGO

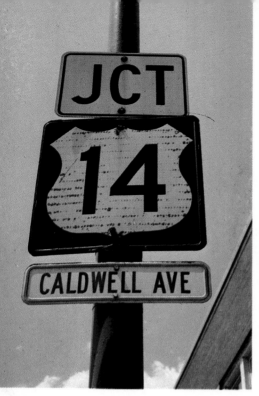

PICTURE CREDITS

Tom Dunnington—7, 8, 10, 11, 12, 14, 19, 21, 22, 23, 24, 27, 28, 32, 33, 34, 35, 43

Colour Library International—18

Ray Hillstrom—2, 41 (center right and left, bottom), 44 (bottom right)

Picture Group—©John Sheckler 13

Historical Picture Services—30

Eric Santi—Cover, 38 (3 photos)

Tony Freeman—4, 41 (top), 44 (bottom left and top)

John Edwards—36, 37

28441

Library of Congress Cataloging in Publication Data

Carona, Philip B.
  Numbers.

  (A New true book)
  Previously published as: The true book
of numbers. 1964.
  Includes index.
  Summary: Explains the development of our
system of numbers, place value, and why numbers
are used.
  1. Numeration—Juvenile literature.
[1. Number systems] I. Title.
QA141.3.C37 1982   513′.2   82-4455
ISBN 0-516-01634-2   AACR2

TABLE OF CONTENTS

4

THE IDEA OF NUMBERS

We use numbers every day.

Try to count the different ways we use numbers.

Your house has a number. Your telephone has a number. Some of the games you play use numbers, too. There are numbers everywhere.

People have not always used numbers as we do.

Long, long ago a caveman may have had two spears.

Perhaps he saw two elephants.

He could see that two spears and two elephants were different. Yet he may have seen that they were alike in one way.

Perhaps he was beginning to get the idea of TWO.

One day he might see
one group of animals on a
hill. There might be
another group of animals
by the river. TWO groups.

The caveman did not
have a word or a number
sign for the idea of TWO.

If he killed two
elephants, he might paint
two elephants on the cave
wall. This was the way he
told how many he had
killed.

NUMBER SIGNS

Slowly people began to understand the idea of numbers. They made up their own number signs. A certain sign stood for a certain number. The sign used for a number is called a numeral.

Many different number
signs have been used.

Here are some of the
number signs that were
used in Egypt 5,000 years
ago.

Egyptian numerals

I = 1	III / III = 6	⌒ = 10
II = 2	IIII / III = 7	⌒I = 11
III = 3		ℓ = 100
IIII = 4	IIII / IIII = 8	ℓ = 1,000
III / II = 5	III / III / III = 9	⌐ = 10,000
		⌒ = 100,000

ℓ 999 / 999 / 999 ⌒⌒ / ⌒⌒ / ⌒⌒ ⌒ II = 1992

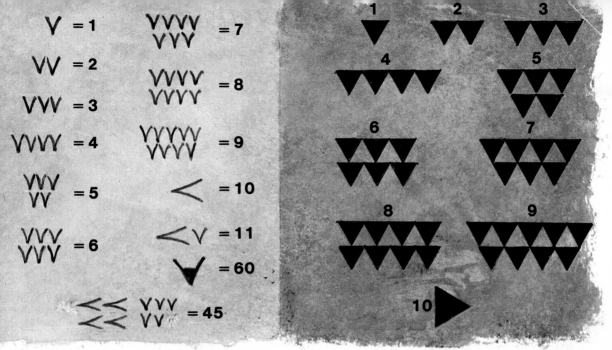

Babylonian numerals   Mesopotamian numerals

About the same time the people in Babylonia made number signs.

They only counted to sixty. So they had a number sign for sixty and started counting all over. This is how they wrote the number seventy-five.

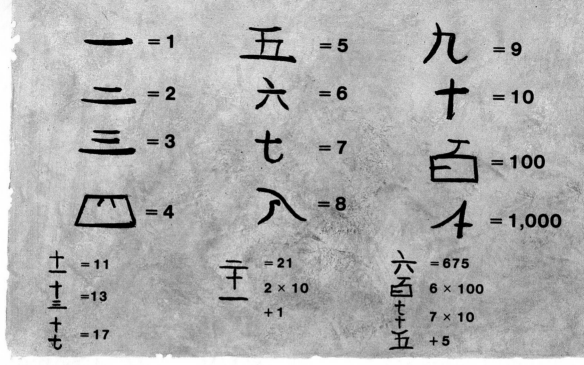

Chinese numerals

The Chinese painted number signs with a brush. They wrote their numbers down a page. This is the number twelve in Chinese.

The Romans made
number signs (numerals)
that are still used. You can
find Roman numerals on
clocks and on buildings.

I—1	X—10
II—2	XI—11
III—3	XII—12
IV—4	XIX—19
V—5	XX—20
VI—6	XXV—25
VII—7	XL—40
VIII—8	XLV—45
IX—9	L—50

The numerals for one, two, and three were just lines. I   II   III

For five they used V.

For ten they used X.

Four is one less than five. So the I was put before the V. One less than five is four or IV.

Six is one more than five. So the one was placed after the five. Five plus one is six or VI.

Ten was a new sign X. Fifty was a new sign L.

L—50
XC—90
C—100
CD—400
D—500
CM—900
M—1000

For larger numbers, the Romans used the first letter of Latin words. The Romans spoke Latin. They took their number signs from their alphabet.

The Latin word for hundred is *centum.* So the letter used for hundred was C.

The letter D was used for five hundred.

The Latin word for thousand is *mille.* So the letter used for thousand was M.

It is not hard to read Roman numerals, but they are clumsy to use.

MCMXCVII stands for 1997.

M=1000   XC=90
CM=900   VII=7

The Maya Indians of
Central America used
number signs. They

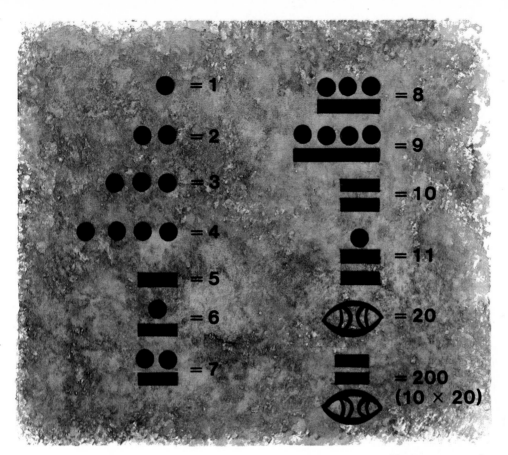

Mayan numerals

counted on their fingers
and toes. So they used a
number system based on
twenty.

Dots and dashes stood
for numbers.

NUMERALS TODAY

Numerals we use look like this:

1   2   3   4   5

6   7   8   9   0

Where did they come from?

Long before the Romans were using letters to express number ideas, people in India were writing numerals. They looked like this.

Indian numerals

The people were called Hindus, and they had nine number signs.

With nine number signs the Hindus could write any numeral.

These numerals were not clumsy.

They were easy to read.

They were easy to work with.

If a man wanted to buy three sheep, he wrote it this way:

3

If he wanted to buy thirty-three sheep, he wrote it this way.

33

Each three had a "place value." Three ones and three tens.

If he wanted to buy three hundred thirty-three sheep, he wrote it this way:

333

Each three had a place, three ones, three tens, and three hundreds.

He had a number
pattern. It was based on
ten.

How could he write
three hundred and three?

There were no tens.

He left a space and
wrote it this way:

3　3

This sometimes led to trouble. If a man wrote a 3 3 he might get only thirty-three because his numeral was hard to read.

As time went on, the Hindus began using a dot to show there was no number in that place. They wrote 3 • 3 and this was better. This means three hundreds, no tens, and three ones.

Later this small dot became a circle. The circle is now called ZERO.

The Hindus had created one of the world's great inventions. It was the numeral zero.

Zero is the number sign that means no quantity— nothing.

The Hindus were traders.
They traveled to many
different countries. When
they traveled they took
both goods and ideas with
them.

They shared their number ideas with the Arabs. The Arabs made some changes. This was the way they wrote their number signs:

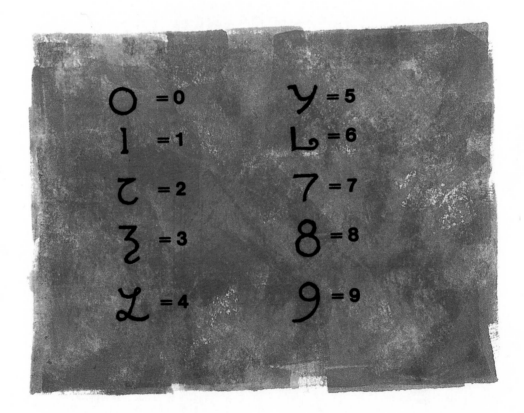

The Arabs carried the ideas farther west. Spain began to use the ten number signs and place value. The numerals were called Arabic numerals. Soon they were used all over Europe.

The shape of the numerals changed many times.

Then, about six hundred years ago, printing was invented.

The shape that numerals took at that time was kept.

These are the numerals that we use today.

We call them Arabic numerals.

WORKING WITH NUMBERS

Long ago people found a way to work with numbers without using any numerals, or number signs. They worked with an abacus. The word abacus comes from the Latin word *abax,* which means tablet.

The early abacus was
made by drawing three
lines in the sand. Pebbles
were placed on the lines.
The pebbles can show
637, when placed this way.

6   3   7

Suppose you have 231 camels and you buy 125 more. How many camels would you have?

This is how you would set the pebbles so they showed 231.

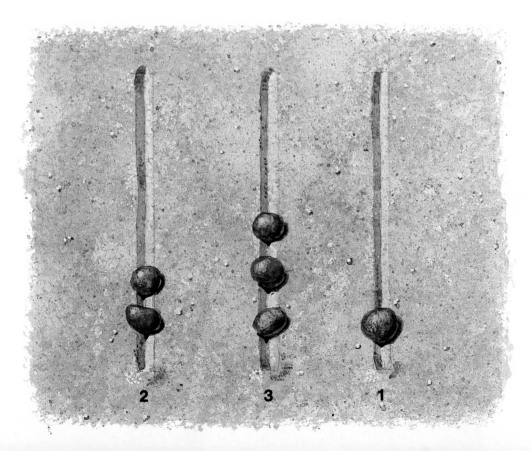

2   3   1

231 + 125 = 356

This is how you would add 125.

First put five pebbles on the line for ones. Put two pebbles on the line for tens. Then put one pebble on the line for hundreds.

Now you can see that you have 356 camels.

Now you have more camels than you want. If you sold forty-five how many would you have left?

Take five pebbles from the line for ones. Take four pebbles from the line for tens. Now you can see that you have 311 camels left.

$$356 - 45 = 311$$

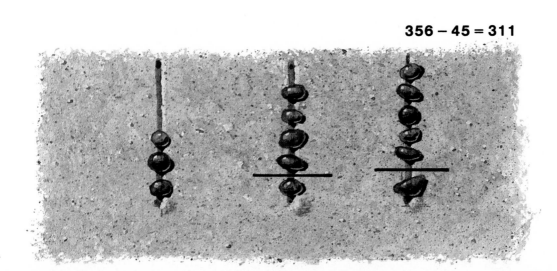

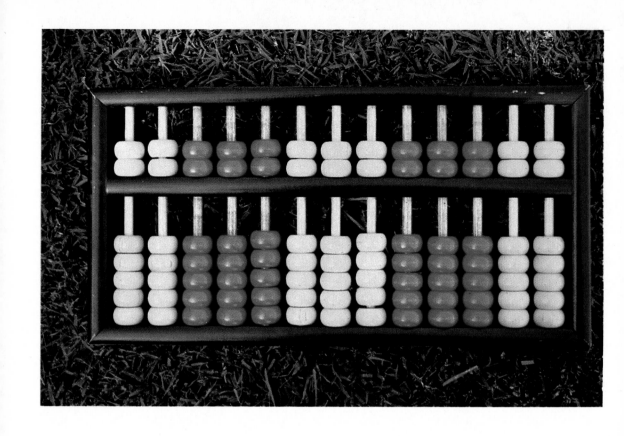

The Chinese use an
abacus that has colored
beads. The beads can be
moved back and forth on
rods.

Even today, some people use an abacus when they are working with numbers.

We use numbers every day.

They tell us how far, how fast, how much, how many, how tall.

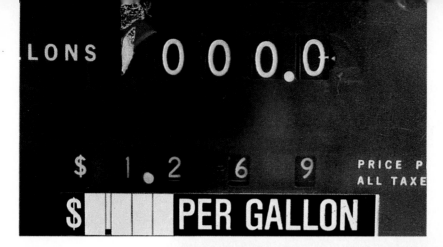

LONS 000.0

$ 1.2 6 9

PRICE P
ALL TAXE

$ PER GALLON

	ABC 2	DEF 3
GHI 4	JKL 5	MNO 6
PRS 7	TUV 8	WXY 9
*	OPERATOR 0	#

956-3550

88 90 92 94 96 98 100

550 600 700

TREBLE BALANCE LOUDNESS

MIN MAX LEFT RIGHT ON OFF

We work with numbers every day... if we use a telephone... bake a cake... play the radio... keep a score... or buy anything. Can you think of other ways we use numbers?

People work with numbers
when they build a bridge...
or design a jet... or find
the height of a mountain
on the moon by measuring
its shadow.

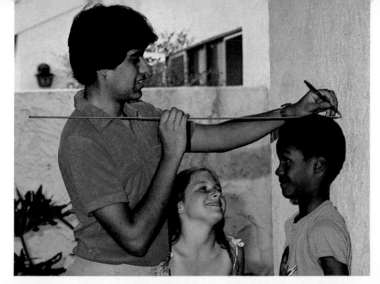

THINGS TO THINK ABOUT

The idea of numbers goes on and on and on, without end.

We use Arabic numerals when we work with numbers.

With these ten number signs we can write symbols for all numbers.

This is because we use PLACE VALUE.

Thousands	Hundreds	Tens	Ones	
			6	Six
		6	0	Sixty
	6	0	0	Six Hundred
6	0	0	0	Six Thousand

Millions	Hundred Thousands	Ten Thousands	Thousands	Hundreds	Tens	Ones	
						2	Two
					2	0	Twenty
				2	0	0	Two Hundred
			2	0	0	0	Two Thousand
		2	0	0	0	0	Twenty Thousand
	2	0	0	0	0	0	Two Hundred Thousand
2	0	0	0	0	0	0	Two Million

Thousands	Hundreds	Tens	Ones

Thousands	Hundreds	Tens	Ones

We use a pattern when we work with numbers. The pattern we use is a base ten. This is not the only pattern, but it is a good one to work with.

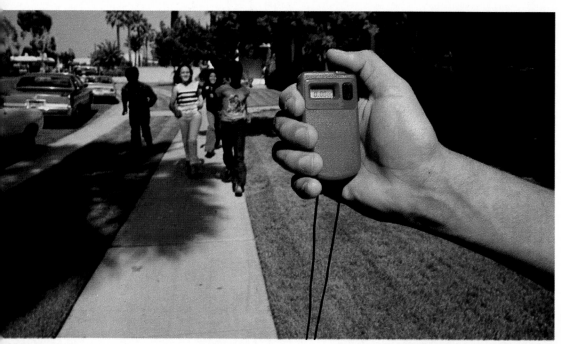

Numbers are interesting.
You can learn to think about numbers.

You can discover things about numbers.

The more you learn to work with numbers, the more exciting they become. You will want to know more about them.

WORDS YOU SHOULD KNOW

Arabs(AIR • abz) —a group of people living in many lands, mainly in southwestern Asia and northern Africa

Babylonia(bab • ih • LONE • ee • ah) —ancient country in southwest Asia

Central America(SEN • tril) —area between Mexico and South America

design(dih • zine) —plan that works as a pattern to follow

Egypt(EE • jipt) —country in northeast Africa

Europe(YOO • rup) —continent west of Asia on the east of the North Atlantic Ocean.

Hindu(HIN • doo) —a people of India

idea(eye • DEE • ah) —plan; thought in the mind

numeral(NOOM • er • el) —a symbol that represents a number

number(NUM • ber) —mark or sign that stands for how many

pattern(PAT • irn) —design, arrangement of something

place(PLAYSS) —in arithmetic a position of a number alone or in a series

sign(SINE) —mark used to stand for or mean something

Spain(SPAYN) —a country in southwestern Europe

symbol(SIM • bul) —something that means or stands for something else

traders(TRAY • ders) —people who sell and buy things

INDEX

About the Author

Philip Carona received his advanced degrees in education from the University of Houston. An experienced teacher and principal, he became director of Elementary Curriculum in the Texas school system. Books by Dr. Carona have been published by Prentice-Hall, Follett, and the U.S. Department of Education.